PENELOPE, OF ITHACA

Kenny Finkle

BROADWAY PLAY PUBLISHING INC
224 E 62nd St, NY, NY 10065
www.broadwayplaypub.com
info@broadwayplaypub.com

First printing: December 2014
I S B N: 978-0-88145-607-3

Book design: Marie Donovan
Page make-up: Adobe Indesign
Typeface: Palatino
Printed and bound in the U S A

PENELOPE, OF ITHACA was first produced by The
Hangar Theatre (Peter Flynn, Artistic Director; Lisa
Bushlow, Executive Director) in Ithaca NY in July 2010.
The cast and creative contributors were:

AUNT PENNY .... Susannah Berryman
ODYSSEUS, TELEMACHUS .... Brian Edelman
PENELOPE .... Kelly Hutchinson
LUCIUS .... David Graham Jones

Director .... Peter Flynn
Scenic designer .... Julia Noulin-Mérat
Costume designer .... Greg Robbins
Lighting designer .... Annie Wiegand
Sound designer .... Eric Watkins
Production manager .... Adam Zonder
Stage manager .... Kerri J Lynch
Casting director .... Judy Bowman
Composer .... John Simon

CHARACTERS & SETTING

PENELOPE
LUCIUS
ODYSSEUS
PEGGY FONTAINE
TELEMACHUS *(played by the actor playing* ODYSSEUS*)*

Time: Now

Place: In and around Ithaca, New York.

NOTE

I wrote this play for a hot summer night.
A romance of longing.
The world of the play is wet, natural, lyrical,
smoldering, woven.
Time is fluid in the play, moving forwards and
backwards without warning,
sometimes moving in both directions at the same time.
Peggy Fontaine is always on stage, watching, guiding,
judging, loving.
Lucius' songs and music are vital to elevating the
world out of realism.

< = overlapping lines.

… = a character either doesn't know what to say or
doesn't want to say what they feel.

For small creatures such as we the vastness is bearable only through love.
Carl Sagan

ACT ONE

(A huge floor loom on one side of the stage. A huge tree on the other side of the stage. Ithaca Falls upstage and a center space that's elevated.)

(LUCIUS sits in the middle on the platform, strumming on his guitar.)

(The first thing we hear is this—his guitar, softly playing. It's an upbeat tune, hopeful, sweet, fun…)

LUCIUS: *(Singing)*
I used to think that true love would never find me
I used to think that I'd be alone all my life
But then I woke up and saw your shining face
I never knew that it all could feel so right

(LUCIUS plays underneath as PEGGY FONTAINE, ancient but spunky, enters cradling a baby in her arms. She's talking to the baby…)

PEGGY: Of course that was a different time in Ithaca. A more magical time. Do you believe in magic? Oh I do, I believe in magic…and love. I believe in love.

(ODYSSEUS and PENELOPE, appear standing together, under the tree. PEGGY hands them their baby—TELEMACHUS. The two completely and utterly in love.)

LUCIUS: Oh you make me blush
When I see you I get a rush
You take me high, there is no low

You are the one that i wanna know and know and know

PENELOPE: He has your eyes.

ODYSSEUS: He has your toes.

PENELOPE: He has your feet.

ODYSSEUS: He has your nose.

PENELOPE: I love you Odysseus Johnson.

ODYSSEUS: I love you Penelope Fontaine Johnson.

PEGGY: *(From her loom—giving instruction)* Now you're going to wind your warp onto the warp beam.

LUCIUS: Your love's like a plane in the sky
Gonna fly higher
Your love's like the water in the sea
Gonna swim deeper
And be free…

(Music continues—strumming and humming…)

PEGGY: You're gonna make mistakes and that's why I'm here. No one expects you to do it right, not just yet, but by the time we're done with your lessons, you'll know more than you ever cared to about weaving. But we're just getting started. This is how we start.

ODYSSEUS: I have some news.

PENELOPE: Yeah?

ODYSSEUS: Yeah. Wanna guess?

PENELOPE: Tell me.

ODYSSEUS: Come on, guess.

PENELOPE: Give me a hint.

ODYSSEUS: What have I been waiting to hear about?

PENELOPE: …No.

ODYSSEUS: Yes…

PENELOPE: Really?

ODYSSEUS: Really.

PENELOPE: Oh baby.

ODYSSEUS: I know.

PENELOPE: When?

ODYSSEUS: Soon.

PENELOPE: How soon?

ODYSSEUS: A month.

PENELOPE: A month? But we just moved in, we—

ODYSSEUS: I know.

PENELOPE: Can't you ask for a—

ODYSSEUS: Nell, I've been waiting for this for a long time, I can't—

PENELOPE: But—

ODYSSEUS: We have this month. We have this month and then later, later—we'll have the rest of our lives and—are you happy for me? Say you're happy for me.

PENELOPE: Of course I am.

ODYSSEUS: I love you, you know that, don't you? You know I love you.

PENELOPE: I know you do.

ODYSSEUS: Do you love me?

PENELOPE: You know I do. It's just—

ODYSSEUS: It's just what?

PENELOPE: What if something happens—what if—

ODYSSEUS: Nothing is ever going to happen to me.

PENELOPE: But you're going to—

ODYSSEUS: No matter what happens I'll come back to you.

PENELOPE: Promise?

ODYSSEUS: Promise. Do you promise to always wait for me?

PENELOPE: Always and forever.

ODYSSEUS: Cool, so we're good?

PENELOPE: Yes we're good.

ODYSSEUS: Good and besides you got Peggy and Lucius here to look after you. Right Lucius, you'll look after Nell when I'm gone?

(LUCIUS *stops playing and turns to them.* PEGGY *continues working having not heard...)*

LUCIUS: You're going somewhere?

ODYSSEUS: Yup. But not just yet. I'm not going anywhere, just yet.

(ODYSSEUS *takes* PENELOPE's *face in his, kissing her, comforting her.* LUCIUS *goes back to playing.)*

LUCIUS:
I've been thinking I've never known what life is
But with you I can forget my past
The only thing that matters to me now
Is getting you
Getting you next to me... (next to me)

PEGGY: Now you are going to bring the thread through the heddles. You're going to do one at a time. You're going to lift the harness and pull a thread through the eye of heddle number one. You're going to do the same for heddle number two and so on and so forth. Are you even listening to me?

PENELOPE: (*Looking dreamily at* ODYSSEUS *and* TELEMACHUS) I'm listening Aunt Peggy, I'm listening.

PEGGY: Are not.

LUCIUS: *(Singing)*
Love's like a plane in the sky
Gonna fly higher
Love's like the water in the sea
Gotta swim deeper
And be free...

And be free.
And be free

And be free.
You and me

(The sound of the waterfall seems to take over as ODYSSEUS *and* PENELOPE *exit in different directions.* PENELOPE *rushes by* LUCIUS *and he follows her giddier, sillier, younger... They are in high school...)*

PENELOPE: I can't see!

LUCIUS: Me neither. Maybe we should turn around.

PENELOPE: No. No way. You said you wanted to do something exciting and coming to Ithaca Falls at night is about as exciting as I can think of in Ithaca, New York.

LUCIUS: It's a little slippery.

PENELOPE: Hold my hand.

LUCIUS: Where are you?

PENELOPE: Right here!

LUCIUS: Right where?

PENELOPE: Here!

*(*LUCIUS *and* PENELOPE *find each other, he grabs her hand.)*

PENELOPE: Your hand is warm.

LUCIUS: So is yours.

PENELOPE: Have we ever held hands before?

LUCIUS: I don't think so.

PENELOPE: Me neither. How long have we known each other?

LUCIUS: Since kindergarten.

PENELOPE: You're my oldest friend. And my best friend Lucius Cammotion.

LUCIUS: You're mine too Penelope.

PENELOPE: We must have held hands back then right?

LUCIUS: I don't remember.

PENELOPE: Me neither. I don't remember anything about kindergarten.

LUCIUS: I do. I remember how we met.

PENELOPE: How'd we meet?

LUCIUS: You told me that all the legoes were yours and to get away from them. And then I cried and gave them to you. And then our teacher Ms Kim came over and sorted everything out and you had to apologize to me.

PENELOPE: I must have hated that.

LUCIUS: You did. After she walked away you told me that you didn't mean it but since Ms Kim was watching, we should pretend like we were playing together.

PENELOPE: Sounds like me doesn't it?

LUCIUS: Yup.

PENELOPE: Do you think I'm a selfish person Lucius?

LUCIUS: I think you have some selfish qualities yes.

PENELOPE: I can't help it. I think its because I'm an only child. And an orphan. Aunt Peggy has spoiled me terribly.

LUCIUS: Well if anyone deserves to be spoiled, its you.

PENELOPE: *(Overly regal)* Yes I agree.

(LUCIUS *and* PENELOPE *giggle.*)

PENELOPE: This is nice. Do you think this is nice?

LUCIUS: Yeah, I do. *(Beat)* Penelope I—

PENELOPE: Listen!

(The waterfall seems to get louder.)

LUCIUS: What?

PENELOPE: The water!

LUCIUS: Oh. Yeah.

PENELOPE: It sounds kind of scary at night.

LUCIUS: You think?

PENELOPE: Yeah, don't you?

LUCIUS: I guess kind of.

PENELOPE: It sounds like danger. I can see why people would think this would be a good place to end it all. Though I can't imagine ever getting the courage to do that, could you?

LUCIUS: No but I don't think that kind of thing is in my nature.

PENELOPE: It's really intense. It's so—alive! I've never been here at night. Have you?

LUCIUS: Nope.

PENELOPE: That's just crazy. We're seventeen years old! We should have been here once at night by now, don't you think?

LUCIUS: I don't know, maybe we weren't supposed to come here until now.

PENELOPE: Yeah, it was meant to be.

(Beat)

LUCIUS: Yeah, P, I wanted to—

PENELOPE: Isn't it crazy that something can be here all
the time making all this sound and we forget about it!

LUCIUS: I guess.

PENELOPE: Oh come on Lucius, think about it.

LUCIUS: I'm thinking about it.

PENELOPE: Are not.

LUCIUS: True.

PENELOPE: Oh my god.

LUCIUS: What?

PENELOPE: We totally left my Aunt's car behind.

PEGGY: Weaving is a very stimulating activity, very
tactile, you'll see. I equate it to sex.

LUCIUS: You're just realizing this now?

PENELOPE: Yeah. Why did we walk here?

LUCIUS: You thought that'd be fun.

PENELOPE: But that means we're gonna have to walk
back to the movie theatre after this!

LUCIUS: It's not that far P.

PENELOPE: Far enough! We should have driven here.

(Appearing out of the darkness, ODYSSEUS *in his underwear
and wet.)*

ODYSSEUS: Naw, its more fun to walk.

PENELOPE: Odysseus Johnson what are you doing here?

LUCIUS: Practically naked no less.

ODYSSEUS: Summer swim. What are you two doing
here?

LUCIUS: Running from the fuzz.

ODYSSEUS: Cool.

PENELOPE: He's just kidding. We just went to the movies and I thought we should come here.

ODYSSEUS: Not as interesting as Lucius' story.

LUCIUS: The truth never is.

ODYSSEUS: True.

PENELOPE: Are you here alone?

ODYSSEUS: Yeah.

LUCIUS: Do you always swim naked alone in Ithaca Falls?

ODYSSEUS: Maybe. And I'm not naked, yet. I still have my underwear on. But not for long. Do you guys wanna smoke up?

PENELOPE: Totally.

LUCIUS: I don't smoke.

PENELOPE: Lucius is a straight edger.

LUCIUS: So were you until like 3 seconds ago.

PENELOPE: I was not.

LUCIUS: Were too and you know it.

ODYSSEUS: Have you ever smoked pot before?

PENELOPE: No.

ODYSSEUS: A virgin. Cool.

PENELOPE: That sounded gross Odysseus.

ODYSSEUS: It did?

LUCIUS: It did.

ODYSSEUS: Didn't mean to. Here.

(ODYSSEUS *hands* PENELOPE *a joint and lights it.* PENELOPE *inhales.*)

PENELOPE: This is really good stuff.

LUCIUS: Like you would know.

ODYSSEUS: It's my Moms.

LUCIUS: You stole marijuana from your Mom?

ODYSSEUS: I didn't steal it. She keeps like tons of it in the freezer, so I just took some. Like taking ice cream or ice or something frozen.

LUCIUS: Aren't you getting cold without any clothes on?

ODYSSEUS: No.

PENELOPE: Are you sure?

ODYSSEUS: *(Looking inside his underwear)* Yeah everything's just hanging out. Take off your clothes and come in with me.

PENELOPE: O K.

LUCIUS: I should probably just go home.

PENELOPE: What's your damage Lucius?

ODYSSEUS: Yeah, what's your damage?

LUCIUS: What's my damage? I don't have any damage. I just don't want to go swimming.

ODYSSEUS: La-ame!

PENELOPE: *(Giggling)* That's not nice Odysseus.

ODYSSEUS: Oh yeah and you asking him what his damage is, is real nice too.

PENELOPE: I'm allowed to be mean to Lucius, he's been my best friend forever.

LUCIUS: P, I think we should head home.

PENELOPE: But I want to swim!

LUCIUS: It's late and your Aunt is gonna—

PENELOPE: I'll find my way home. Odysseus will take me home, right?

ODYSSEUS: No.

PENELOPE: No?

ODYSSEUS: I'm not going home for hours and hours.

PENELOPE: Why not?

ODYSSEUS: Because I'm up to no good.

PENELOPE: Like what?

ODYSSEUS: Like something seriously exciting.

PENELOPE: Like what?

ODYSSEUS: Like if I tell you, you both have to promise never to tell anyone ever.

PENELOPE: I promise.

ODYSSEUS: Lucius?

LUCIUS: I promise.

ODYSSEUS: I don't believe you Lucius.

LUCIUS: I promise.

PENELOPE: He's good at keeping promises. And secrets. You can trust him.

ODYSSEUS: But this is bigger than whatever secrets or promises you've ever kept before.

LUCIUS: Maybe I should just go then.

ODYSSEUS: Maybe you should.

PENELOPE: Why are you being so mean to him Odysseus?

ODYSSEUS: Because like I said, I don't trust him.

PENELOPE: Well how can Lucius prove to you that he's trustworthy?

ODYSSEUS: By taking all his clothes off and smoking some pot and jumping into the water with us.

LUCIUS: I don't want to do any of that.

ODYSSEUS: Are you gay Lucius?

PENELOPE: Oh my god, I can't believe you just asked that!

LUCIUS: No I'm not gay Odysseus. Are you?

ODYSSEUS: I can be a little gay sometimes.

PENELOPE: You sleep with guys?

ODYSSEUS: Sometimes.

PENELOPE: Really?

ODYSSEUS: Not really. But I would if it felt right. I don't judge or anything like that. Are you guys a couple?

PENELOPE: No.

ODYSSEUS: Are you sure?

PENELOPE: I think I'd know.

ODYSSEUS: Lucius are you guys a couple?

LUCIUS: You heard what Penelope said.

ODYSSEUS: I just wondered if maybe you felt differently.

LUCIUS: We're not a couple.

ODYSSEUS: O K, if you say so. So come on you guys, take off your clothes, come in the water and I'll tell you guys my big secret plan to break into Carl Sagan's house tonight.

PENELOPE: You're planning on breaking into Carl Sagan's house?

ODYSSEUS: Yup.

PENELOPE: Why?

ODYSSEUS: Because Carl Sagan is rad and I want to steal something from his office.

PENELOPE: What do you want to steal?

ODYSSEUS: I don't know, something cool. I'm ready to go back in the water. You guys coming?

PENELOPE: I'm coming.

ODYSSEUS: Lucius?

LUCIUS: I don't know.

ODYSSEUS: Well I'm going back in.

(ODYSSEUS *turns around, pulls his underwear off and jumps into the water. We hear the splash.*)

(PENELOPE *starts taking her clothes off.*)

PENELOPE: Come on Lucius! We wanted an adventure and here's an adventure! Come on.

LUCIUS: I don't feel comfortable here.

PENELOPE: What's the big deal?

LUCIUS: The big deal is that I thought we were going to be alone and Odysseus is kind of—

PENELOPE: Wonderful. Don't you think he's wonderful?

LUCIUS: No. No I don't. I think he's dangerous and—

PENELOPE: Yeah, isn't that wonderful?

LUCIUS: No I don't think its wonderful, I think its— dangerous.

PENELOPE: I think you're over-reacting.

LUCIUS: I think you're not listening to me. Penelope listen I want to tell you that—

PENELOPE: I'm sorry Lucius. You're right, I'm just—I'm kind of stoned now and Odysseus—O K, Odysseus is—I've never told you this but I have such a crush on Odysseus Johnson I can not handle it. I think he's so hot. Do you think he's into me? I can't tell. He's very aloof. But so interesting. I've always thought he was interesting. Have you ever seeing him running? He's a beautiful runner. He has such a beautiful body. Like a God. He runs everywhere, I think he's like a long

distance runner or something. He's always running
with his shirt off, except in the winter duh, then he has
a shirt on, but he totally runs by my house all the time.
I love watching him run. Even Aunt Peggy who's as
dykey as they come, has to catch her breath when he
runs by the house.

PEGGY: Oh yes, I had my lesbian years here in Ithaca.
Happens to everyone that comes here. I believe
something comes in from the falls.

PENELOPE: I'm going to try to kiss him tonight. Or get
him to kiss me I mean. No one has ever kissed me
Lucius and tonight is the night! I can feel it! I think you
should totally either come in the water right now or
you should go so I can be alone with Odysseus. I mean,
I don't want to be rude or anything but you're kind
of being a buzzkill and that's—I'm being rude. We're
still best friends, this is just—like—I don't know—I'm
having a total experience right now.

ODYSSEUS: *(From the falls)* Hey, you two, stop jabbering
and come in already!

(Beat)

PENELOPE: Well?

*(LUCIUS turns away and is gone. PENELOPE is just about to
take her clothes off and head into the Falls when—)*

PEGGY: Now Penelope you are going to feel your warp
and make sure it is taut.

(PENELOPE goes to PEGGY and the loom.)

PENELOPE: How do I—

PEGGY: Play it like a harp. Go on, feel it and tell me, is
it taut?

(PENELOPE feels the warp.)

PENELOPE: It seems taut.

PEGGY: Could it be tauter?

PENELOPE: I don't know.

PEGGY: What is there to know? It either could be tauter or it could not.

PEGGY: Honestly, Penelope, focus. Focus!

PENELOPE: I'm focusing!

PEGGY: Are not. I'll never get through the fundamentals of weaving with you at this rate. I promised your mother, god rest her soul, that I'd teach you all my secrets and pass on all my knowledge and expertise but you're so wiggly we can't get past steps one and two. And even when we do, it takes me so long to get you back here after a lesson, all the work I've done to teach you has come undone and we have start back at the beginning again. I should have taught you earlier, when you were a little girl but you were so damn cute I didn't want to fence you in with learning a vocation. This is all my fault for spoiling you silly, so I take the burden but damn it Penelope you must apply yourself! Now feel the damn warp and tell me what you think.

(PENELOPE *does. She pulls again. She thinks. She does one more time.*)

PENELOPE: I guess I'd like it a little tauter.

PEGGY: Good. Now how are you going to do that?

PENELOPE: I don't know.

PEGGY: Then figure it out. You're almost a grown woman, its time you started figuring things out for yourself. Go on. Attack this with gusto Penelope. Attack it! I do everything in my life with gusto. I'm a dynamo. Always have been. Don't be afraid to make mistakes. Mistakes are wonderful. My whole life practically has been mistakes and I'm the better for it and so is my weaving!

(During the following PENELOPE *is figuring out how to tighten the warp.)*

PEGGY: *(Helping* PENELOPE *along)* You are very very cold right now. Warmer. Warmer still. There you go. There's the hot spot. You got it.

Now tighten it.

PENELOPE: I'm done.

PEGGY: Let me see then. *(She tests it.)*

PEGGY: Oh my you like things wound up now don't you!

PENELOPE: I thought—I guess I thought that—

PEGGY: No I like that. I like that a lot. That's a surprising new revelation in your character Penelope Fontaine. You like things wound up tight. That's good. Very good. Now we're getting somewhere! Next, you're going to—

*(*ODYSSEUS *appears.)*

ODYSSEUS: Nell.

*(*PENELOPE *stands up to go to* ODYSSEUS.*)*

PEGGY: Sit back down Penelope.

*(*PENELOPE *sits.)*

ODYSSEUS: Nell!

*(*PENELOPE *is back up.)*

PEGGY: Sit.

*(*PENELOPE *sits.)*

ODYSSEUS: NELL!

*(*PENELOPE *rushes to* ODYSSEUS.*)*

ODYSSEUS: I didn't think you heard me.

PENELOPE: I had to wait until my Aunt was asleep.

ODYSSEUS: I thought maybe you stopped loving me.

PENELOPE: Never. I'll never stop loving you.

ODYSSEUS: I'll never stop loving you either. I want to ask you something.

PENELOPE: Then ask me.

ODYSSEUS: Not here.

PENELOPE: Why not?

ODYSSEUS: Because…come on!

(ODYSSEUS *pulls* PENELOPE. *As he does,* PEGGY *calls her back*—ODYSSEUS *is gone.*)

PEGGY: Earth to Penelope, earth to Penelope, come in Penelope.

PENELOPE: I'm right here Aunt Peggy.

PEGGY: Your body may have been here but your mind was not. Now sit back on the bench.

(PENELOPE *does.*)

PEGGY: Move the treadles.

PENELOPE: The treadles?

PEGGY: Right there. Like pedals on a piano. See em?

PENELOPE: Yes.

PEGGY: Go on, step on one.

(PENELOPE *does. The loom moves—one row of thread rises while another falls.*)

PENELOPE: Oh!

PEGGY: Exciting isn't it? I remember the first time I saw the thread separate, it is something of a small joy. And that of course is what life is all about—the small joys. Didn't know you were going to be learning life lessons here from old Aunt Peggy Fontaine did you? I can't help it, when you get to my age, the wisdom just flows like water from a spigot.

PENELOPE: Odysseus Johnson asked me to marry him and I said yes.

PEGGY: ...See that space there? That's where you're going to move your yarn through when we get to that. But not today. Today is all about fundamentals.
Go back to Odysseus and tell him no.

PENELOPE: But—

PEGGY: But nothing. Tell him he must first ask me for permission to ask for your hand.

And tell him he should come sooner than later.

PENELOPE: Why's that?

PEGGY: Because Penelope you are pregnant and time is ticking on by.

PENELOPE: How did you—

PEGGY: When you get to my age you can just sense these things.

(PEGGY *turns around and confronts* ODYSSEUS, *who has just appeared.* PENELOPE *stands behind him.*)

PEGGY: Speak.

ODYSSEUS: Um, Ms Fontaine,

PEGGY: The name is Peggy and you know it, you've called me Peggy every day for the past two and a half years you've been courting my niece so why now are you calling me Ms Fontaine?

ODYSSEUS: Um—because—you told Penelope that you wanted this to be proper so—

PEGGY: *(To* PENELOPE*)* Can't you get anything right? *(Back to* ODYSSEUS*)* What I said was I am responsible for Penelope and her mother and father god rest their souls would not approve if I didn't make sure Penelope and her potential husband went through proper procedures in these matters. Penelope's parents

were very old fashioned. Wonderful people whom
I'm sorry you won't get to know. You would have
adored them and they my boy would have adored you.
Penelope's father, was a runner like you. A man among
men he was. If Penelope's mother hadn't scooped him
up, I would have had that man for breakfast, lunch,
dinner and a midnight snack. Now go on with what
you came for.

ODYSSEUS: So Peggy I'd like to ask for permission to
have Penelope's hand in marriage.

PEGGY: You just want to marry her hand?

ODYSSEUS: No. That's a phrase I—

PEGGY: I know it's a phrase I was making a funny. I'm
known to do that from time to time. So you want to
marry Penelope.

ODYSSEUS: Yes.

PEGGY: And how do you intend to provide for her?

PENELOPE: Aunt Peggy, please—

PEGGY: You be quiet. I'm in the midst of an
interrogation here young lady. Answer my question
Odysseus.

ODYSSEUS: Well right now I'm working at Ithaca
Bakery but only for a little while longer.

PEGGY: And why's that?

ODYSSEUS: Because—

PENELOPE: Because he has some other offers for other
jobs and—

PEGGY: What kind of other jobs?

PENELOPE: Good ones.

PEGGY: Didn't I tell you to hush? What kind of jobs
Odysseus?

ODYSSEUS: Well there's...I'm sorry Penelope.

PEGGY: What are you sorry for?

ODYSSEUS: Penelope told me that I shouldn't tell you this.

PEGGY: Tell me what?

ODYSSEUS: I've been recruited by the Army.

PEGGY: I beg your pardon.

ODYSSEUS: The Army they've recruited me.

PEGGY: The Army? As in the Army of the United States?

ODYSSEUS: Yup. Special Ops. Some guy saw me doing one of my long distance runs and was impressed and had me come in for some tests a couple months back and I guess I was off the charts, now I'm just waiting for a call to basic training.

PEGGY: When?

ODYSSEUS: Whenever they call me. He said it could be anywhere from tomorrow or a year from now.

PEGGY: I never thought of you as a warrior Odysseus.

ODYSSEUS: Me neither but it turns out I am. They said they'd never seen someone more suited for the kind of work they do. They went through all this stuff we'd be doing and it really got me excited.

PEGGY: Excited for what?

ODYSSEUS: To...fight.

PEGGY: Fight what?

ODYSSEUS: Injustice. There are terrible things happening all around the world.

PEGGY: I read the paper every day Odysseus, I know what's going on around the world.

ODYSSEUS: Well then you know why I'm excited. I can make a difference.

PEGGY: There are a lot of ways you can make a difference and not all of them include joining the Army.

ODYSSEUS: Out there is where I'm going to be used best.

PEGGY: How do you know that?

ODYSSEUS: Because I can feel it.

PEGGY: You can feel it.

ODYSSEUS: It's easy to make this sound naïve.

PEGGY: This is naïve. You're young, you don't know. You haven't lived through war before. You don't know what war does to people. I do. Do you have any idea what it means to join an army young man?

ODYSSEUS: I—I think I do.

PEGGY: Well you don't. And you— (To PENELOPE) this makes you happy?

PENELOPE: It's what Odysseus wants.

PEGGY: But does it make you happy?

PENELOPE: If Odysseus is happy, I'm happy. Who am I to stand in the way of that?

PEGGY: His future wife, the mother of his child, that's who you are. Do you have any idea what it means to be the wife of someone in the army?

PENELOPE: We've talked through all of this Aunt Peggy. We—

PEGGY: Are children. That's what you are. Children... Sit down. Both of you. Sit.

(ODYSSEUS and PENELOPE do. Beat. PEGGY looks at them, sternly.)

PEGGY: Penelope knows this but you don't and its high time you did…I am the Original Wild Woman of Ithaca.

ODYSSEUS: The Original Wild Woman of Ithaca?

PEGGY: Oh yes. Everyone will tell you. Go on and ask people. They'll tell you—I've fought to preserve the quality of this fine city all my adult life. I've fought the big fights, I've walked the walk, I haven't always won but winning isn't the point, it's the fight that matters. The fight! I've fought the infiltration of big business, I demanded new school curricula, I've fought for solar energy and to keep the trees up near Cornell and not to turn the whole damn city into a parking lot, I've lead rallies, organized demonstrations, staged sit ins, made giant peace signs that planes could see flying by. I'm the reason that Ithaca is the way it is…except for the bad things, I'm not responsible for those. But even those I suppose I allowed so I must take responsibility for them too. What I'm trying to get at is I know what it means to need to fight enemies Odysseus, to feel that there's injustice and wrong in the world but if you want to fight, stay here and fight for things that will impact your wife and your child and your child's children. Fight here. We could fight together Odysseus. We could—

ODYSSEUS: And if I don't?

PEGGY: Well for one, you will not have my blessing on your marriage.

PENELOPE: Aunt Peggy?!

(PENELOPE *grabs* ODYSSEUS' *hand and pulls her from* PEGGY, *disappearing, as* LUCIUS *appears playing his guitar, trying to write a song.*)

PEGGY: Get back here you two this conversation is not finished. Get back here now.

LUCIUS: *(Singing)* Love!
(Spoken) No too much.

PEGGY: PENELOPE! PENELOPE!! *(Surprisingly winded, sits at her loom.)*

LUCIUS: *(Quieter)* Love.
(Spoken) Better.
(Singing) Love falls like a rain.
*(Spoken)*Yuck.

PEGGY: Old. I'm getting old quick. PENELOPE? *(She starts to work.)*

LUCIUS: *(Singing the* All You Need is Love*)*
Love
Love
Love
(Spoken) Someone wrote that already.
(Singing) Your love is like a plane in the sky…

PEGGY: She's not here.

LUCIUS: Where is she?

PEGGY: Got me.

LUCIUS: Did she say when she'd be back?

PEGGY: No.

LUCIUS: Will you let her know I stopped by?

PEGGY: I will.

(PENELOPE appears. PEGGY stands.)

LUCIUS/PEGGY: Penelope.

PENELOPE: Hi.

PEGGY: You did it didn't you?

PENELOPE: Yes.

LUCIUS: Did what?

PENELOPE: I—we—

PEGGY: She eloped with Odysseus.

LUCIUS: Eloped? *(He walks off.)*

PENELOPE: Odysseus Johnson is the love of my life and I had to marry him whether you approved or not. Do you hate me Aunt Peggy?

PEGGY: Come here.

(PENELOPE does.)

PEGGY: I'm not going to stop loving you. I'm not going to shut you out. I said what I had to say about it. It's your life young lady to do with as you see fit.

(PEGGY cups PENELOPE's face in her hands.)

PEGGY: Too quick. Too quick! I know I'm holding your face too long but I want to take you in one last time like this.

PENELOPE: You say that like something is about to happen to me.

PEGGY: Life is about to happen to you young lady and I want to remember this last moment of innocence, even if you are knocked up and you eloped, you are still an innocent.

PENELOPE: I don't feel like an innocent.

PEGGY: I know you don't. But from my vantage point you are the most innocent creature to ever walk the earth. Life is going to test you Penelope, are you ready for it?

PENELOPE: I don't know what I'm ready for.

PEGGY: That's what I was afraid of. And that's why I've got to teach you to weave.

PENELOPE: But I don't want to weave.

PEGGY: What do you want to do?

PENELOPE: I don't know.

PEGGY: Well until you know, you'll weave.

PENELOPE: But—

PEGGY: But nothing. Weaving will always be here for you if you let it. When you need to get away, when you need to think, when you need to dream, when you need to cry, weaving will be here for you. Long after I'm gone, weaving will be here. *(She lets go of* PENELOPE's *face.)*

PEGGY: Now sit down and let's continue lessons.

(Before PENELOPE *even sits,* LUCIUS *appears.)*

LUCIUS: Penelope.

PENELOPE: *(Looking up)* Lucius!

PEGGY: Keep you eyes on the loom Penelope.

LUCIUS: Come here. I wanna show you something.

PENELOPE: What is it?

LUCIUS: Just something. Come on.

*(*LUCIUS *holds out his hand,* PENELOPE *takes it and he pulls her up.)*

LUCIUS: Close your eyes.

PENELOPE: Why?

LUCIUS: Because I have a surprise for you.

PENELOPE: I don't like surprises.

LUCIUS: You do too. Close your eyes.

PENELOPE: Oh O K.

*(*PENELOPE *closes her eyes while* LUCIUS *moves to the tree.)*

LUCIUS: O K, P, on three! Ready?

PENELOPE: O K, on three.

LUCIUS: One. Two. Three! Open your eyes!

(LUCIUS *turns the tree into a beautiful bed made in and from the tree.*)

PENELOPE: Oh my god.

LUCIUS: Do you like it?

PENELOPE: How did you do this?

LUCIUS: You know I was thinking about preserving nature and also I snuck into that lecture at Cornell last year about solar energy and I thought this was the coolest idea—to just—you know, build the bed and the bedroom right around the tree. And see I built in a glass ceiling there so you can see the leaves on the tree and—

PENELOPE: Oh Lucius, this is—I'm—oh wow. *(She falls onto the bed. Rolls around on it)*

PENELOPE: Does it suit me?

LUCIUS: Like a glove… So you like it?

PENELOPE: Do I like it? Lucius—I—I love it. Thank you. But this isn't what we—we can't afford to pay you for this, we're—

LUCIUS: It's my gift to you. For getting married. Since you didn't have a wedding, I mean, since you didn't invite anyone to your wedding, I didn't get to give you anything and so—this is—a gift.

PENELOPE: Oh Lucius, that's—thank you. Thank you thank you thank you thank you thank you thank you thank you.

LUCIUS: You're welcome you're welcome you're welcome you're welcome you're welcome you're welcome.

(Offstage the sound of a baby crying. PEGGY pulls the baby seemingly out of the loom, wrapped in a beautiful woven blanket. She holds the baby, cradling him, trying to get him to quiet down.)

PEGGY *goes back to weaving…* LUCIUS *is gone. It is now late at night.)*

ODYSSEUS: Penelope?

*(*PENELOPE *lying in bed wakes up with a start.)*

PENELOPE: Odysseus?

ODYSSEUS: Hey babe.

PENELOPE: You're back? When'd you get back?

ODYSSEUS: Just now.

PENELOPE: You should have called. I would have been up. I would have made you some food, I would have—

ODYSSEUS: I wanted to surprise you.

PENELOPE: Where have you been?

ODYSSEUS: I can't tell you.

PENELOPE: Why not?

ODYSSEUS: Secret. Secret missions.

PENELOPE: But I'm your wife, we're not supposed to have secrets.

ODYSSEUS: This is it, our only secret.

PENELOPE: Can't you at least tell me something?

ODYSSEUS: I was far away.

PENELOPE: How far?

ODYSSEUS: Really far.

PENELOPE: Across the world?

ODYSSEUS: Farther than that.

PENELOPE: Farther than that?

ODYSSEUS: Farther than that.

PENELOPE: Was it dangerous.

ODYSSEUS: Very.

PENELOPE: Were you scared?

ODYSSEUS: Very.

PENELOPE: Did you win?

ODYSSEUS: Yes.

PENELOPE: Did you miss me?

ODYSSEUS: Yes.

PENELOPE: I missed you too Odysseus. So much has
been happening here. Telemachus is growing. Fast.
Like every day he's bigger. And Aunt Peggy had
a stroke. A little stroke. We didn't even know she
had one until one afternoon a few weeks ago when I
noticed her hands were shaking when she was putting
thread onto the loom. We went to the Doctor and they
did some tests and that's how we found out. Are you
back for good now Odysseus?

ODYSSEUS: Yeah.

PENELOPE: Good. ...Come to bed baby.

ODYSSEUS: Uh uh, you come here.

PENELOPE: Why?

ODYSSEUS: Because I said so.

PENELOPE: The bed is warm.

ODYSSEUS: So are my arms. Come on Nell, come to me.

PENELOPE: Why do you tease me?

ODYSSEUS: Because I can.

PENELOPE: Come on just get into bed with me.

ODYSSEUS: No, you come to me.

PENELOPE: You're lucky you're irresistible.

ODYSSEUS: I know.

(PENELOPE *gets out of bed,* ODYSSEUS *runs off.)*

PENELOPE: Where are you going Odysseus?

ODYSSEUS: Try to catch me.

PENELOPE: Odysseus I don't want to play games.

ODYSSEUS: But I do. Come on Nell, catch me. *(He runs off.)*

PENELOPE: Odysseus? ...Odysseus, this isn't funny. *(She wanders the space looking for her husband. She wanders to the waterfall.)* Odysseus?

(LUCIUS appears out of the darkness.)

LUCIUS: Penelope.

PENELOPE: Lucius! You scared me. What are you doing here?

LUCIUS: You called me.

PENELOPE: I did?

LUCIUS: You asked me to meet you here, remember?

PENELOPE: ...I did. I'm sorry, I don't know what I'm doing anymore Lucius. I think I'm losing my mind! A year and a half Lucius! A year and a half and not a word! Not a sign. Nothing. I've been told to stop calling and asking for updates. But I can't help it. I can't help thinking that something will happen and if I don't call they'll forget to call me. Sometimes I think I—you're going to think I'm ridiculous—

LUCIUS: I'd never think you were ridiculous P.

PENELOPE: I know you guys haven't really— Odysseus hasn't ever really been nice to you. I know he hasn't. But that's because he's jealous. He's jealous because we've known each other forever and forever and we have a bond that he can't understand. But he will, when he gets back, you and he will spend more time together. You'll get to know him and he'll get to know you and you two will become great friends. I just know you will.

(LUCIUS *is silent.*)

PENELOPE: Oh my god, I just had the greatest idea ever.

LUCIUS: What's that?

PENELOPE: You should move in with me and
Telemachus!

LUCIUS: Move in?

PENELOPE: Sure, wouldn't that be fun?

LUCIUS: I have a place to live.

PENELOPE: Yeah but you're all alone there.

LUCIUS: I like living alone.

PENELOPE: You do not.

LUCIUS: I do too.

PENELOPE: You act like you're a loner but you're not.
You like people. You like being around people.

LUCIUS: I only like being around certain people.

PENELOPE: Well I know you like being around me. And
I know you love Telemachus. You're so good with him.
We could—you could—we would kind of be raising
him together for a while. Just until Odysseus gets back.

LUCIUS: I don't know P. I don't think that's—

PENELOPE: Oh come on, you know you want to! Then
we can hang out whenever we want.

LUCIUS: We already hang out all the time.

PENELOPE: But this way I wouldn't even have to
call you. At least not on the phone. I could just go—
LUCIUS! And you'd be there.

LUCIUS: Maybe I wouldn't answer.

PENELOPE: You always answer me.

LUCIUS: True.

PENELOPE: Oh come on, it'd be fun. We could go grocery shopping together. Wouldn't that be fun? To go to Wegman's together and run down the aisles with our list. I got the raspberries!

LUCIUS: I got the grapefruit!

PENELOPE: I got the garlic!

LUCIUS: I got bread!

PENELOPE: You got multi-grain right? I don't want Telemachus to ever taste white bread.

LUCIUS: Yup, I got multi grain. Should I get some chicken for tonight?

PENELOPE: Yes chicken for tonight and for tomorrow get a couple tuna steaks.

LUCIUS: I could get some mangoes and make a chutney to go with them.

PENELOPE: That sounds delicious!

LUCIUS: Is it your night to cook or mine?

PENELOPE: Tonight is supposed to be yours but we can switch if you want.

LUCIUS: Do you like to cook?

PENELOPE: I love to cook. Do you?

LUCIUS: I love it too.

PENELOPE: Odysseus doesn't cook. He likes me to cook for him. Which I like to do but it would be fun to cook with you. We could bake things too. Aunt Peggy gave me a delicious chocolate banana bread recipe I've been dying to try out but I haven't had anyone to share it with.

LUCIUS: I'll share it with you P.

(Beat. Then resuming the role playing)

PENELOPE: Will you put Telemachus to bed tonight?

LUCIUS: Yup.

PENELOPE: I'm going to take a bath.

LUCIUS: I got you some great new bubble bath.

PENELOPE: What kind?

LUCIUS: Eucalyptus.

PENELOPE: I love eucalyptus.

LUCIUS: I know.

PENELOPE: You know me so well.

LUCIUS: You know me so well too.

PENELOPE: We could share everything Lucius. It would be non stop happiness all the time. And I need happiness, I'm so lonely in the house. It needs someone else there with me and Telemachus and we have the room.

What do you think?

LUCIUS: I—I can't.

PENELOPE: Why not?

LUCIUS: Because I can't…

PENELOPE: I don't understand, I—

LUCIUS: Penelope I—I just need for there to be—I need—my own space. That's all.

PENELOPE: But—

LUCIUS: Penelope I love you. Don't you know that? That I love you.

PENELOPE: I love you too Lucius.

LUCIUS: Not the same way. Not like I love you. I love you the way you love Odysseus. I always have. I think I've felt this way since we were five years old. That night we came here. The night you and Odysseus…I was going to tell you but then... And I thought at one time that you did too.

PENELOPE: I, —I, no, no I haven't, I—

LUCIUS: Even when we were younger? Even then?

PENELOPE: ...maybe then. Before Odysseus. Maybe I did then. Maybe then I thought you and me were going to be together forever.

LUCIUS: We still can be. We can be together. Me and you.

PENELOPE: No we can't. Not now.

LUCIUS: We can now. We can be together.

PENELOPE: I'm with Odysseus.

LUCIUS: Odysseus is never coming back Penelope!

PENELOPE: Yes he is!

LUCIUS: He's been missing for a year and a half P, a year and a half!. Missing. There's no way, he's—

PENELOPE: He's going to come back to me Lucius. He promised he would. He promised. He'll come back. And how dare you suggest otherwise! I thought you supported me! I thought you believed like I believed, I thought—

LUCIUS: Kiss me P. Kiss me.

PENELOPE: No.

LUCIUS: Just one kiss and if after that you don't—

PENELOPE: No.

LUCIUS: Just one and then we can—

PENELOPE: No.

LUCIUS: What's wrong with me that you don't want to kiss me?

PENELOPE: Nothing's wrong with you Lucius.

LUCIUS: I feel like something is wrong with me. Do you think I'm disgusting? Do you hate me?

PENELOPE: No Lucius, no, I don't—I don't know what I—

LUCIUS: Then kiss me.

PENELOPE: Lucius—

LUCIUS: What if I just grabbed you and took you, would you submit then? Would you give in to my kisses then?

PENELOPE: No.

LUCIUS: I don't believe you.

PENELOPE: You're scaring me.

LUCIUS: I'm gonna take you.

PENELOPE: Stop it.   LUCIUS: I'm gonna—

(LUCIUS *grabs* PENELOPE *and kisses her. She resists violently, then gives in, fully, and then just as quickly pulls away.*)

LUCIUS: Why are you pulling away? You felt that, you felt it, I know you did.

PENELOPE: I don't know what I felt. I—I'm confused. I'm—

LUCIUS: You're not confused, you're scared. I'm scared too. We can be scared together. We can—>

PENELOPE: < I still love him, I still hope he'll come back, I still wait >

LUCIUS: < Let me help you get over him, let me help you—>

PENELOPE: < This is—too much. You're—too much. Aunt Peggy! ?

(PENELOPE *runs through the space looking for* PEGGY. LUCIUS *chases after her.*)

LUCIUS: Penelope!

PENELOPE: AUNT PEGGY!!!!!

LUCIUS: PENELOPE!!!!

(PEGGY *appears.*)

PEGGY: What is it child?

LUCIUS: PENELOPE TURN AROUND AND LOOK AT ME!

PENELOPE: I'm ready now. Teach me. Teach me how to weave. Show me your secrets. Show me everything. Show me. Now. Please. Now.

PEGGY: We're going to have to start back at the beginning you know.

PENELOPE: I know. I know.

LUCIUS: PENELOPE!

PEGGY: And you'll have to stay focused this time.

PENELOPE: I will.

LUCIUS: Penelope?

(ODYSSEUS *appears, deep in war.*)

ODYSSEUS: Penelope.

PEGGY: From the beginning.

LUCIUS: I'll wait P.

ODYSSEUS: Wait for me.

LUCIUS: I'll wait for as long as you tell me to wait.

PEGGY: This young lady is a floor loom.

ODYSSEUS: Will you wait for me?

PEGGY: It belongs to me now but previously it was my mother's and before that my grandmother's and before that her mother's.

LUCIUS: I'll wait. And I'll be here.

LUCIUS/ODYSSEUS: I'll never love any one the way I love you.

PEGGY: It is an old Fontaine heirloom and one day it will be yours.

LUCIUS: I'll wait until you're ready. I'll wait.

LUCIUS/ODYSSEUS: Do you hear me?

LUCIUS: I'll wait. I'll be patient.

ODYSSEUS: Be patient.

LUCIUS: I can be patient.

PEGGY: For the time being we will share this until I feel you have mastered the art form.

LUCIUS: I can be the most patient man that ever lived.

ODYSSEUS: Can you hear me Penelope?

PEGGY: Now sit. We have a lot of work to do.

PENELOPE: Aunt Peggy?

PEGGY: I know. I know all that you're feeling. Put it into your work and you'll see, beautiful things will emerge. Beautiful things. Go on now. Sit.

(PENELOPE *sits.* LUCIUS *goes to his guitar and starts playing…*)

LUCIUS: (*Singing—insistent/driving rhythm*)
I want a spell that makes time not hurt
Four tons of patience
Twenty gallons of ice
Mix it with some loneliness
Just to give it some bite

ODYSSEUS: Penelope?

LUCIUS: (*Singing*) Cast it over me

ODYSSEUS: Penelope?

LUCIUS: (*Singiing*) Let me feel numb

ODYSSEUS: PENELOPE!

LUCIUS: Let me forget who I'm waiting for
Let time run
Let time run
Let time run

PEGGY: Good. Now. What shall we weave first?

(Blackout)

END OF ACT ONE

ACT TWO

(In darkness, the chords from Let Time Run*)*

(Lights up on LUCIUS, *playing his guitar, his voice has gotten more urgent, as if he's been singing this song non stop for years…)*

LUCIUS: Let time run!

(Lights up on ODYSSEUS, *high above and far away.)*

ODYSSEUS: Penelope.

(Lights up on PENELOPE *looking up at* ODYSSEUS.*)*

PENELOPE: Odysseus!

LUCIUS: *(Singing)* Let time run!

ODYSSEUS: Can you hear me?

PENELOPE: Yes. Can you hear me?

LUCIUS: *(Singing)* Let time run!

(Light up on PEGGY *standing by the loom.)*

PEGGY: You must get to your heart Penelope.

PENELOPE: My heart.

LUCIUS: *(Singing)* Let time run!

PEGGY: What is in your heart?

PENELOPE: What is in my heart?

LUCIUS: *(Singing)* Let time run!

PEGGY: Wait for it.

ODYSSEUS: Are you there?

PENELOPE: I'm here. Odysseus? Odysseus!

LUCIUS: *(Singing)* Let time run!

PENELOPE: Nineteen years Odysseus! Nineteen years!

(ODYSSEUS disappears.)

PEGGY: Go deeper.

PENELOPE: Nothing. Nothing else is in my heart.

LUCIUS: *(Singing)* Let time run!

PEGGY: Dig.

PENELOPE: I can't.

PEGGY: Breathe.

PENELOPE: I can't.

LUCIUS: *(Singing)* Let time run!

PEGGY: Breathe when you can't breathe.

PENELOPE: Breathe when I can't breathe.

PEGGY & PENELOPE: And dig.

LUCIUS: *(Singing)* Let time run!

(PENELOPE sees LUCIUS. He starts strumming So Wrong of Me*...a real ballad.)*

PENELOPE: Lucius.

(As LUCIUS continues to play, she walks to him.)

LUCIUS: It's been a long time P.

PEGGY: Deep.

LUCIUS: Eighteen years.

PENELOPE: I know.

LUCIUS: I'd given up. Kind of. I never really gave up. I just—I'm glad to see you.

PENELOPE: I'm glad to see you too. I saw you at Peggy's funeral.

LUCIUS: I figured you did.

(Light up on TELEMACHUS, *20, spitting image of his father.)*

TELEMACHUS: Peggy Fontaine died as she lived.

PENELOPE: *(To* PEGGY*)*

I can't breathe.

TELEMACHUS: She always told us she was dying. Every day.

PEGGY: Deeper.

TELEMACHUS: But we never believed her.

PENELOPE: I'll never finish anything.

PEGGY: Don't think about finishing.

PENELOPE: But I have to sell things. I have to make money. I have to—

TELEMACHUS: And then she was just gone.

LUCIUS: *(Singing)* I still do miss you

PEGGY: Your job is to dig.

LUCIUS: *(Singing)* I don't know how

PENELOPE: My job is to put food on the table.

LUCIUS: *(Singing)* All this time waiting
For something that won't ever come about

PEGGY: I've provided you with money, haven't I?

PENELOPE: For now.

LUCIUS: *(Singing)* I've been so lonesome and sad

PEGGY: Enough for now. Your job is to dig.

LUCIUS: *(Singing)* I know that I have it bad.

PENELOPE: I can't do it.

LUCIUS: *(Singing)* But nobody understands

PEGGY: Yes you can.

LUCIUS: *(Singing)* Where you are now.

PEGGY: GO!

(PEGGY *leads* PENELOPE *back to the loom.)*

LUCIUS: *(Singing)* I'm gonna wait for you forever
I know somehow you're coming home
Waiting is part of the pleasure
Or maybe I'm just gonna roam and roam and roam

PENELOPE: I'm no good.

PEGGY: Yes you are.

PENELOPE: There's nothing down there.

PEGGY: Yes there is. Bravery!

PENELOPE: I'm not brave.

PEGGY: You can be.

PENELOPE: I don't want to be brave.

PEGGY: You have no choice. Look at your life.

PENELOPE: *(To* LUCIUS*)* You should have come by after.
You—

LUCIUS: I didn't want to make things weird.

PENELOPE: It wouldn't have been weird. It would have
been right. You knew Peggy. You loved her, you—

LUCIUS: I meant for you and you know it. And it would
have been weird. I saw Telemachus speak.

TELEMACHUS: My great Aunt Peggy was the most
important person in my life.

PEGGY: I'm glad you spoke about me.

TELEMACHUS: She was my moral compass.

PEGGY: You and me—we knew each other. Didn't we?
But now you can't hear me. Look at her. My Penelope.

PENELOPE: *(To* PEGGY*)* I can't breathe.

PEGGY: Hold her Telemachus. Hold her and tell her you love her.

LUCIUS: *(Singing)* Oh its so wrong of me
To hold on so tightly
And its so bad of me
To think you'd even care

PENELOPE: I'm lost.

PEGGY: You don't know if you love her. She's not been a good mother to you. Too hot or too cold. And you— you're perfectly warm. You need warmth. And I—I need—>

TELEMACHUS: < I—I can't do this. This is too hard. *(He runs off.)*

PEGGY/PENELOPE: Telemachus!

PEGGY: You've pulled everything tight Penelope, now you have to let it go.

PENELOPE: How do I do that?

PEGGY: You just do.

(PENELOPE back at her loom. Trying to figure it out...)

LUCIUS: *(Singing)* Oh, its so wrong of me
To hold on so tightly
And its so bad of me
To think you'd even care
But when i think of you I get caught up in it
Oh its so wrong of me
But it feels so right

(End of song. LUCIUS looks to PENELOPE. She gets up from her loom, comes to him during the following.)

LUCIUS: You look—

PENELOPE: Old.

LUCIUS: I was gonna say good.

PENELOPE: Good and old.

LUCIUS: If you're old, I'm old.

PENELOPE: You're old.

LUCIUS: Older. I'm older.

PENELOPE: You've grown into—you're a man now Lucius.

LUCIUS: …I don't want to be weird or anything but I've seen you around town over the years. I haven't stalked you or anything creepy like that, but I've seen you at places, with Peggy and Telemachus or by yourself. I used to walk by you at the Farmer's Market. You were sitting there weaving or selling stuff and I'd just walk by…

PENELOPE: I know.

LUCIUS: You saw me too?

PENELOPE: Yes. Saw you, heard about you, Ithaca isn't a big place, you know.

LUCIUS: So I suppose you probably know all about what's been going on in my life?

PENELOPE: Peggy kept tabs. She'd casually report things to me while we were working.

PEGGY: There wasn't anything casual about it at all. I'd report things to you purposely and clearly.

LUCIUS: So you know I was married.

PENELOPE: And divorced.

LUCIUS: You know I left for a bit.

PENELOPE: A year. You left for a year.

LUCIUS: Do you know where I went?

PENELOPE: You rode a bike around the country.

LUCIUS: Yeah.

PENELOPE: Why'd you do that?

LUCIUS: I have no idea. Stupidest thing I've ever done. Hated every minute of it...What else do you know about me?

PENELOPE: I know you live out here in Aurora now. In this big old house that you're fixing up nice and slow... too slow for a lot of your neighbors...you build things for people, you stay to yourself, mostly, I guess a couple years ago there was a woman out in Skaneateles you were courting but it didn't last long according to Peggy...

PEGGY: It was about six months, if I recall and then she ran off with her best friend's father.

PENELOPE: You have a garden full of delicious vegetables—the best variety anyone has ever seen, you stay up late a lot and play your guitar and watch the stars and...you ask about me.

LUCIUS: I'm pretty transparent huh?

PENELOPE: I like that about you.

LUCIUS: I hate that about myself.

PENELOPE: I know you do.

PEGGY: Let it go Penelope. Let it all go. Open yourself up to possibility.

PENELOPE: Do you write songs or do you play other people's?

LUCIUS: Both I guess. I write stuff of my own from time to time.

PENELOPE: Would you play me one of yours?

LUCIUS: Maybe.

PENELOPE: Why just maybe?

LUCIUS: Because maybe I will and maybe I won't. We'll just have to see.

PENELOPE: See what?

LUCIUS: Just see. That's all.

(Beat)

PEGGY: You've stopped breathing again.

(TELEMACHUS *appears.)*

TELEMACHUS: Mom.

(Snapped out of LUCIUS, *who is gone, she goes back to her loom, trying to work.)*

PENELOPE: What is it Telemachus?

TELEMACHUS: I need some money.

PENELOPE: Why don't you have any of your own?

TELEMACHUS: I lost my job.

PENELOPE: You lost your job?

TELEMACHUS: Ok, I let it lose me.

PENELOPE: Telemachus you can't keep going from job to job, you have to find something you love and apply yourself.

TELEMACHUS: Thanks for the sage wisdom.

PENELOPE: I wish you wouldn't talk to me like that.

TELEMACHUS: I wish you wouldn't talk to me like that either.

PENELOPE: I'm your Mother Telemachus, I—

TELEMACHUS: —you what?

PENELOPE: You should listen to me and respect me and—

TELEMACHUS: —Look Mom let's not do this, you and I both know you have never been much of a mother to me, that was Peggy's job and she's gone now so let's just keep it real here ok?

PENELOPE: Telemachus, I wish you wouldn't—

TELEMACHUS: What. Tell the truth. This is the truth Mom. You've spent my entire life either locked up in your studio trying to make something or locked up in your room trying to—I don't know what, so you and me? We're not—anything.

PENELOPE: I'm trying to work Telemachus.

TELEMACHUS: Can I have some money?

PENELOPE: …I don't have any money to give you.

TELEMACHUS: You do too.

PENELOPE: No Telemachus I don't.

TELEMACHUS: What about Peggy's money?

PENELOPE: What about it?

TELEMACHUS: Where is that?

PENELOPE: In the bank.

TELEMACHUS: So go to the bank and get some money.

PENELOPE: I'm working Telemachus and you're 20 years old. You need to make your own money.

TELEMACHUS: So do you. Have you ever sold anything of your own?

PENELOPE: That's— Get out.

TELEMACHUS: Mom, I didn't mean to—I—

PENELOPE: GET OUT. NOW.

TELEMACHUS: Mom, please I—

PENELOPE: I'll never finish anything if I keep getting interrupted.

TELEMACHUS: Sure Mom, if you want to use me as your excuse.

PENELOPE: I'm not using you as—

TELEMACHUS: Whatever.

(TELEMACHUS *turns and finds himself face to face with* LUCIUS.)

LUCIUS: You must be Telemachus.

TELEMACHUS: I know you.

LUCIUS: You do?

TELEMACHUS: You're that guy who built that house for the movie star up the lake.

LUCIUS: Lucius. My name is Lucius.

TELEMACHUS: Lucius what?

LUCIUS: Lucius Cammotion.

TELEMACHUS: That's a weird name.

LUCIUS: So is Telemachus.

TELEMACHUS: My name means "decisive battle". Does your name mean anything?

LUCIUS: Not that I'm aware of.

TELEMACHUS: My Dad, Odysseus named me.

LUCIUS: I know.

TELEMACHUS: How do you know that?

LUCIUS: Because I knew your Dad.

TELEMACHUS: From where?

LUCIUS: From here. We all went to school together. Me, your mom, your Dad,

TELEMACHUS: Then why is this the first time I've seen you here?

LUCIUS: I've been here before. When you were a baby. I used to hold you in my arms.

TELEMACHUS: That doesn't count.

LUCIUS: Counts to me.

TELEMACHUS: Where have you been all this time then?

LUCIUS: Aurora.

TELEMACHUS: Why?

LUCIUS: Because that's where I live now.

TELEMACHUS: Why?

LUCIUS: That's—complicated.

TELEMACHUS: What are you doing here now then?

LUCIUS: What is this—twenty questions?

TELEMACHUS: Yes. We never have people over. And this is my house. I'd like to know what some strange guy is doing in my house.

LUCIUS: ...Visiting with your Mom. We went hiking today. Over at Buttermilk Falls.

TELEMACHUS: My Mom went hiking?

LUCIUS: Yeah. Have you done that hike before?

TELEMACHUS: Like a million times.

LUCIUS: I haven't done it in years. It was a hot day...

TELEMACHUS: ...Where is my Mom?

LUCIUS: In the kitchen.

TELEMACHUS: I didn't think she even knew where that was.

LUCIUS: She seemed to find it alright.

TELEMACHUS: Shocker.

LUCIUS: If I recall your Mom was a good cook.

TELEMACHUS: Well you recall wrong, my mom hasn't cooked a thing in her entire life. Aunt Peggy used to do all the cooking.

LUCIUS: I'm sorry about your Aunt.

TELEMACHUS: She wasn't my Aunt, she was my Great Aunt.

LUCIUS: I know. I loved Peggy Fontaine.

TELEMACHUS: Take a number.

LUCIUS: That's no way to respond son.

TELEMACHUS: Don't call me son. I'm not your son.

LUCIUS: That was a phrase Telemachus, I didn't mean—

TELEMACHUS: You think I've never heard that phrase before?

LUCIUS: Didn't sound like it.

TELEMACHUS: Well I have.

LUCIUS: I built this house you know.

TELEMACHUS: Seriously?

LUCIUS: Seriously.

TELEMACHUS: Well you did a shitty job. The place is practically falling apart.

LUCIUS: What exactly is falling apart?

TELEMACHUS: Everything. When it rains, we flood. Literally floods in here. And the driveway isn't big enough to get a car into and that floods too when it rains. And the bathrooms are all screwed up and the stairs are rickety and there's not enough closet space in most of the bedrooms, we lost our house plate, so no one can ever find us, our address, it just flew off one day and I could just go on and on if you want…

LUCIUS: This was my first house so—

TELEMACHUS: Yeah, well it shows.

LUCIUS: You think you could do better?

TELEMACHUS: In my sleep.

(PENELOPE *pulls a couple bottles of wine and two glasses out of the loom and enters…*)

PENELOPE: I couldn't decide between a merlot or chardonnay so I brought them both and figured we could drink them both—Telemachus.

TELEMACHUS: Hello Mother.

PENELOPE: You've met Lucius.

TELEMACHUS: I have.

PENELOPE: ...We're old friends from school.

LUCIUS: Telemachus was just telling me that there are a lot of things that need fixing around here.

PENELOPE: Oh, well, things, there are some problems yeah.

LUCIUS: You should have said something earlier P, I would have—

TELEMACHUS: P? You call my Mom P?

LUCIUS: That's what I've always called her. When we were kids and—

TELEMACHUS: I thought you said Dad called you Nell.

PENELOPE: Your father *does call* me Nell but—

LUCIUS:—to me your Mom has always been—P.

(Beat)

LUCIUS: Your mom tells me you're looking for work.

TELEMACHUS: Actually I'm not. I'm not looking.

PENELOPE: You found a job?

TELEMACHUS: No. And I'm not looking for one.

LUCIUS: What are you doing then?

TELEMACHUS: You're looking at it....

PENELOPE: Telemachus thinks he's owed some time off.

TELEMACHUS: That's not true Mom. I just haven't found anything I like yet.

LUCIUS: You said you thought you could do a better job on this house than me, let's see if you're right. I could hire you to fix up this house with me.

PENELOPE: Lucius, we don't have money to—

LUCIUS: It's O K, P, I—

TELEMACHUS: How much would you pay me?

LUCIUS: We'll come to some mutually acceptable number.

TELEMACHUS: Twenty five dollars an hour.

PENELOPE: Telemachus!

LUCIUS: That's not a mutually acceptable number.

TELEMACHUS: That's a number I can live with though. And I know you can afford it.

LUCIUS: And how do you know that?

TELEMACHUS: I heard you made a butt load of money from that movie star house and then you turned around and bought that shit can of a house in Aurora. So I'm figuring you're sitting on cash.

LUCIUS: Is that what you figure?

TELEMACHUS: Yeah.

LUCIUS: Ten dollars an hour.

TELEMACHUS: Twenty two.

LUCIUS: You see the way this works, is from here on—I go down.

TELEMACHUS: And I walk away. See ya.

LUCIUS: Alright, I'll tell you what—fourteen dollars an hour.

TELEMACHUS: You must really want me to work with you.

LUCIUS: I guess I do Telemachus.

TELEMACHUS: Why?

LUCIUS: ...I guess I'm taking an interest in you.

TELEMACHUS: That sounds creepy.

LUCIUS: I don't mean it to be.

(Beat)

TELEMACHUS: Eighteen dollars an hour.

LUCIUS: Sixteen dollars and you have a deal.

TELEMACHUS: Guarantee me twenty hours of work a week.

LUCIUS: Let's see how this project goes and we'll go from there, deal?

TELEMACHUS: No. Twenty hours of work a week on this project and then we'll go from there...deal?

PENELOPE: Telemachus, this is your house, you shouldn't—

TELEMACHUS: He's the one that offered.

LUCIUS: He's right P. I did offer.

TELEMACHUS: So do we have a deal?

(PEGGY *at the loom*)

PEGGY: Penelope!

LUCIUS: ...We have a deal. We'll start first thing tomorrow morning. Nine A M sharp.

TELEMACHUS: First thing for me is noon.

LUCIUS: Well tomorrow, it'll be nine.

PEGGY: Come over here and see what you've done!

PENELOPE: With what?

PEGGY: With this! Come here.

TELEMACHUS: Fine. Tomorrow. 9 A M. Yes sir! See ya!

(TELEMACHUS *is gone.* PENELOPE *goes to* PEGGY. LUCIUS *pulls out tools and has started to work on the house.*)

PEGGY: Look at this.

(*Beat.* PEGGY *and* PENELOPE *look at whatever is on the loom together.*)

PENELOPE: What am I looking at?

PEGGY: You tell me. Look at it. Step back. Take a breath and look.

PENELOPE: (*Looking at her work intently*) Oh.

PEGGY: Very interesting.

PENELOPE: I put my warp color—

PEGGY: Into your weft.

PENELOPE: I'm mixing things up.

PEGGY: Is that on purpose?

PENELOPE: I don't know. I wasn't thinking. I wasn't— it's bad isn't it? I should undo it and start again.

PEGGY: It's up to you.

PENELOPE: I wish you would tell me.

PEGGY: I can't do that anymore.

PENELOPE: Why did I do that? I know which is which. Why did I switch them?

PEGGY: So which color do you want where?

PENELOPE: I don't know what I'm doing with this.

PEGGY: Sit and figure it out.

(*Beat.* PENELOPE *looks at her loom, then sits and gets to work.* TELEMACHUS *enters, tired, and goes to* LUCIUS.)

LUCIUS: You're late.

TELEMACHUS: I told you, I'm not a morning person.

LUCIUS: This is the third time you've been late.

TELEMACHUS: So fire me. I don't care.

LUCIUS: I'm not going to fire you Telemachus, but I am going to deduct it from your pay.

PENELOPE: *(To* PEGGY*)* He's good with Telemachus.

PEGGY: Lucius is good for him. He needs guidance, structure.

TELEMACHUS: Whatever.

LUCIUS: I just want you to apply yourself. You've been doing really well.

TELEMACHUS: I have not.

LUCIUS: You have to. You fixed that banister yesterday without my help at all.

TELEMACHUS: Big deal.

LUCIUS: It is a big deal. That showed some real skill.

TELEMACHUS: I did alright I guess.

LUCIUS: You did.

TELEMACHUS: Did you notice I replaced the newel post?

LUCIUS: I did Telemachus.

TELEMACHUS: I thought it'd be cool to put one in that looked like it fit here.

LUCIUS: I like what you chose.

TELEMACHUS: Yeah me too…

PENELOPE: The other day I heard them talking about me.

PEGGY: What'd they say?

(Another day…)

TELEMACHUS: She never talks about my Dad. Sometimes I think she forgets him.

LUCIUS: I'm sure she hasn't forgotten him.

TELEMACHUS: Then why wouldn't she talk about him?

LUCIUS: Maybe it's just hard for her to.

TELEMACHUS: When I was younger she'd talk to me about him all the time.

(We're back in time. PENELOPE *and* TELEMACHUS *look at each other.)*

PENELOPE: Your father went off to war.

TELEMACHUS: Why?

PENELOPE: To help people who needed help.

TELEMACHUS: Why?

PENELOPE: Because he was asked to.

TELEMACHUS: Why?

PENELOPE: Because your father is special.

TELEMACHUS: Why?

PENELOPE: Because he can do things that other people can't.

TELEMACHUS: Like what?

PENELOPE: Like run fast, and think fast and he's strong and passionate.

TELEMACHUS: What does passionate mean?

PENELOPE: Passionate means he lives his life full of love.

TELEMACHUS: I want to be passionate too then.

PENELOPE: You already are passionate.

TELEMACHUS: I am?

PENELOPE: You are. You know why you are?

TELEMACHUS: Why?

PENELOPE: Because you're his son. And my son too. *(She hugs him.)* I love you Odysseus.

TELEMACHUS: You just called me Odysseus.

PENELOPE: I did?

TELEMACHUS: You did.

PENELOPE: You just—you look so much like him, sometimes I—

TELEMACHUS: Are you O K Mom?

PENELOPE: …I have to go upstairs for a minute… (*She rushes to her bed, crawls in, curls up.*)

(PEGGY *at* PENELOPE's *door*)

PEGGY: Penelope? Penelope, it's been three days…you can't stay in there forever you know. There's food by the door. You got to eat. I'm walking away now, O K? O K… (*She walks to* TELEMACHUS.) What are you doing out of bed you little munchkin?

TELEMACHUS: I couldn't sleep.

PEGGY: You know what used to help me go to sleep when I couldn't?

TELEMACHUS: What?

PEGGY: Chocolate pudding.

TELEMACHUS: Really?

PEGGY: Oh yes. It's a time old Fontaine tradition. Wanna come into the kitchen with me and eat some pudding?

TELEMACHUS: Yes ma'am…

PEGGY: I thought that's what you'd say. Come on.

(PEGGY *and* TELEMACHUS *moving to the kitchen*)

TELEMACHUS: Aunt Peggy?

PEGGY: What is it child?

TELEMACHUS: Does my Mom hate me?

(PEGGY looks at TELEMACHUS as we find ourselves back in the present. PENELOPE watches from her bed.)

LUCIUS: She doesn't hate you.

PENELOPE: Sometimes I do hate him Peggy.

PEGGY: It's not hate, it's fear.

PENELOPE: What am I afraid of?

PEGGY: You tell me.

TELEMACHUS: If she could, she'd trade me to have Dad back.

LUCIUS/PENELOPE: That's not true.

TELEMACHUS: It's how I feel.

LUCIUS: That's a terrible way to feel Telemachus.

(Beat)

LUCIUS: Well, I love you Telemachus.

PENELOPE: I wish I could say that to him.

PEGGY: You can.

PENELOPE: I can't. Not now. It's too late.

PEGGY: It's never too late.

PENELOPE: I feel like it is.

TELEMACHUS: You don't even know me.

LUCIUS: Yes I do.

PEGGY: You can't bottle it up forever.

TELEMACHUS: No you don't. I'm just some guy you knew when he was a baby.

LUCIUS: You're still a baby.

TELEMACHUS: Compared to you old man.

PEGGY: It must come out.

LUCIUS: This is true. But you got a lot to learn Telemachus.

PEGGY: Let it out Penelope.

TELEMACHUS: I…hate it when you get all fatherly with me.

LUCIUS: You do not.

PEGGY: Let it go.

TELEMACHUS: Do too.

PEGGY: Let it all go.

LUCIUS: Do not.

PENELOPE: Let it go. Breathe. Work. Deep. Dig. Bravery.

(PENELOPE *takes a deep breath and the whole world of the play changes for a moment. The sound of the waterfall gets louder—it's presence takes focus. She gets up and walks to it.*)

PEGGY: Yes. Go! GO!

PENELOPE: What is this?

PEGGY: Don't ask questions! Go! GO! GO!

PENELOPE: I want to—dive into it, I want to—

PEGGY: YES!

PENELOPE: Oh Aunt Peggy! This is—

PEGGY: YES!

PENELOPE: (*Overwhelmed*) I—I—can't breathe, I—

PEGGY: Breathe when you can't breathe! BREATHE! GO! GO!

TELEMACHUS: Just be a few minutes ma'am.

(*Quite suddenly,* LUCIUS *and* TELEMACHUS *enter into* PENELOPE'S *work space.* LUCIUS *with a paper bag and his tools.* TELEMACHUS *with his tool belt…*PENELOPE *is pulled back into "reality"…*PEGGY *stays up at the Falls…*)

PENELOPE: (*Disoriented*) What?

TELEMACHUS: I'm pretending like we're workers.

LUCIUS: Don't take it personally, he calls me Boss Man.

TELEMACHUS: I find its best to keep work as impersonal as possible.

LUCIUS: *(Seeing what* PENELOPE *is making)* Wow.

PENELOPE: Wow what?

LUCIUS: Look at that.

PENELOPE: It's nothing.

LUCIUS: It's definitely something.

PENELOPE: I don't know what it is yet. I—I've been trying to do something—I don't know, I'm probably just gonna scrap it soon.

LUCIUS: No. Don't do that. It's good P. It's really good.

PENELOPE: Do you think?

LUCIUS: Yeah. I mean, I don't know anything about weaving but something about this is—yeah, it's—yeah.

PENELOPE: Thank you Lucius…I needed to hear that. I've been having a hard time…forever. I—you know, I never finish anything. I get lost in the pattern or I make the warp too short or weave too tightly. At the Farmer's Market, we always sell Peggy's stuff. She made a lot of things and so that's what I sell there. Not my own.
Telemachus, what do you think of what I'm making?

TELEMACHUS: It's—I like it Mom. It feels like you.

PENELOPE: Whoever that is.

TELEMACHUS: It's good. It's different. It's—I like it.

(Beat)

PENELOPE: So! What do I owe the pleasure of both of you right now?

LUCIUS: We're here to fix that window of yours—

TELEMACHUS: —Ma'am.

PENELOPE: Well it's about time Workmen! That draft is killing me.

LUCIUS: We're real sorry about that.

TELEMACHUS: That's why we brought you a present.

PENELOPE: A present?

TELEMACHUS: Show her!

(LUCIUS *pulls out a cup of Gimme coffee.*)

PENELOPE: Ooh Gimme coffee! (*She takes the coffee and sips.*) Ooh! Did you put caramel in here?

LUCIUS: Six shots of it,

TELEMACHUS: —like you like.

PENELOPE: How did you—

LUCIUS: Don't look at me, Telemachus is the one that—

PENELOPE: I can't believe you remembered that Telemachus.

TELEMACHUS: You used to always ask for that when we went out together. When I was little. So…yeah…

PENELOPE: …Thank you.

LUCIUS: Telemachus, go work on the window.

TELEMACHUS: You see how he talks to me? That's why I call him Boss Man.

(*Beat. A moment of true happiness passes between them… *PEGGY* speaking from the Falls, crossing to the loom as *LUCIUS, PENELOPE *and *TELEMACHUS *find themselves at dinner—the main event, done, empty plates, several bottles of wine— A real feast.*)

PEGGY: Hello people of Ithaca!!!! My name is Peggy Fontaine, as if none of you already knew that. As you can see I'm sitting outside in the middle of the Commons with my floor loom in the middle of

February, in the midst of a cold snap with my niece Penelope Fontaine Johnson and her son Telemachus!

TELEMACHUS: *(At the table)* How old was I when we did that?

PENELOPE: You were almost six.

TELEMACHUS: Why did we do that?

PENELOPE: You don't remember?

TELEMACHUS: I don't. How in the world did we get the big floor loom there?

PENELOPE: Your Great Aunt carried it.

PEGGY: I did not!

TELEMACHUS: She carried the entire thing?

PENELOPE: Yes, she just put it on her back and carried it down to the Commons.

PEGGY: Penelope! How can you say that? That's a terrible way to let him imagine me. We took that damn thing apart and reassembled it and you know it!

TELEMACHUS: Did we do that a lot?

PENELOPE: Nope. Just that once. That one time. We did it for your father.

PEGGY: We did it for you Penelope.

(We're now back in time, PENELOPE turns to PEGGY, gets up, TELEMACHUS follows.)

PENELOPE: I wish we wouldn't do this Aunt Peggy.

PEGGY: Oh hush your mouth. You can't just mope in the house about this.

TELEMACHUS: Mom, I'm cold.

PENELOPE: I'm cold too.

PEGGY: You think I'm not cold! We're all cold. That's the damn point! Now be quiet, here I go.

Now you may be asking yourself what in the world
is this crazy old lady doing out here freezing her
behind off sitting at her damn loom. That's good.
You should be wondering. We want you to wonder.
More than wonder, we want you to remember. That
includes you over there Betty, don't try to duck into
the bank without me noticing. I may be old but I got
eyes like a hawk! As many of you know Penelope's
husband Odysseus went to war five years ago. Five
years ago today. So in honor of that and in honor of the
thousands of men and women who have gone to wars
all around the world, I have moved my weaving studio
out here for the day and I invite you all to weave with
me and my niece Penelope and wait for her husband's
return with us. I invite you to weave with us and pay
respect to the people who have risked their lives for
ours. That's your cue Telemachus.

TELEMACHUS: Please weave with my Aunt and my
Mom! And for my Dad, Odysseus, who I miss very
much, even though I never really met him, that I can
remember!

PEGGY: Good boy. Penelope?

PENELOPE: We have several table looms set up and
ready to go. So please come and weave with me. No
one will be turned away.

LUCIUS: *(Breaking into the memory)* Did anyone come
weave with you?

PENELOPE: It's Ithaca. Of course we had people come
weave with us. We had people there all day.

PEGGY: Eventually I had to shut us down or we would
have gone all damn night too!

(TELEMACHUS *holding up his glass)*

TELEMACHUS: To Great Aunt Peggy!

LUCIUS/PENELOPE: To Great Aunt Peggy!

(The three clink glasses.)

PEGGY: I wish I could hold on to you all right now. I wish I could touch you and feel you and tell you I love you. Soak it all up while you can!

(Beat)

LUCIUS: So Penelope. I'm wondering about something.

PENELOPE: What?

TELEMACHUS: Lucius, don't.

LUCIUS: It's fine.

TELEMACHUS: It's not—

PENELOPE: What is it?

LUCIUS: Well we're almost done with the house. There's some leaks coming in from the roof. Practically in every room upstairs and so I'm wondering if maybe there's some leaking in your room?

PENELOPE: My room?

LUCIUS: Your bedroom.

TELEMACHUS: I told him I didn't know because you never let me in there.

PENELOPE: I—my room is fine.

LUCIUS: Are you sure? Because I could go in there and check things out.

PENELOPE: It's fine. My bedroom is fine.

LUCIUS: Because it'd just take a minute for—

PENELOPE:—Lucius I just told you my bedroom is fine and it's fine. There's nothing to fix in there.

TELEMACHUS: Told you.

PENELOPE: Told you what?

TELEMACHUS: That you wouldn't let him go in there.

PENELOPE: It's not that I won't let anyone in my room Telemachus, it's that there's nothing to fix in my room.

TELEMACHUS: Whatever.

PENELOPE: Not whatever, that's the story. O K? End of story.

TELEMACHUS: And like I said—whatever.

PENELOPE: Do you have something you need to say to me Telemachus?

TELEMACHUS: Nope. I think I said it.

PENELOPE: Because it doesn't sound like you did.

TELEMACHUS: No Mom I said it, you just don't want to hear it.

PENELOPE: I don't know what you—

TELEMACHUS: All I said to Lucius was that I've never been in your bedroom. That the door is shut all day and at night you lock it from inside and that you told me that I am never under any circumstances allowed to go into your room. That's all I said to Lucius and then Lucius said to me that he built that room and that he was sure you'd let him into the room he built and I said to him, I didn't think so because why would you let him into your room and not me and that's all I said. So he thought he'd ask which I thought was a bad idea but he thought he'd do it anyway and now I'm sure he can see that it was a bad idea and >

(Overlapping)

PENELOPE: < It's my room. It's—the only place I have that's just mine and—

TELEMACHUS: Fine, I got it! We got it! You need your privacy, we got it! >

PENELOPE: < Don't you need your privacy? Do I ever go into your room?

TELEMACHUS: You used to. When I was little you would.

PENELOPE: I don't now, because it's your room. You're practically a grown man, you deserve privacy and so do I and—>

TELEMACHUS: < O K! O K! WE GOT IT MOM! YOU NEED YOUR PRIVACY! >

PENELOPE: < Don't raise your voice to me! >

TELEMACHUS: < I'M NOT!

LUCIUS: Telemachus you don't have to—

TELEMACHUS: Don't tell me what I do and don't have to do. *(He exits.)*

PENELOPE: TELEMACHUS! *(She shakes the table with fury.)*

LUCIUS: Hey. Hey P, hey. Stop that. Stop.

(LUCIUS grabs PENELOPE and tries to subdue her. She doesn't let him and then does. She hugs him.)

PENELOPE: He makes me so—

LUCIUS: He doesn't mean to,

PENELOPE: But he does.

LUCIUS: You two are—

(LUCIUS and PENELOPE look at each other.)

(Long beat)

PENELOPE: He called me once.

LUCIUS: Who did?

PENELOPE: Odysseus. I heard from him once. In the middle of the night. Ten, twelve years ago, maybe longer, I've lost count now.

(We hear a phone ring. ODYSSEUS somewhere far away and high appears. LUCIUS is gone.)

ODYSSEUS: Nell?

PENELOPE: Odysseus?

ODYSSEUS: Nell!

PENELOPE: Is it really you?

ODYSSEUS: It's really me!

PENELOPE: Where are you?

ODYSSEUS: Far away.

PENELOPE: When are you coming back?

ODYSSEUS: I don't know.

PENELOPE: Soon?

ODYSSEUS: I don't know.

PENELOPE: It's been so long.

ODYSSEUS: What?

PENELOPE: It's been so long!

ODYSSEUS: Four years! FOUR YEARS, Four months and—

ODYSSEUS & PENELOPE: Twelve days!

ODYSSEUS: I miss you so much Nell!

PENELOPE: I dream of you.

ODYSSEUS: I talk to you all the time!

PENELOPE: I hear you. I hear every word. When are you coming home?

ODYSSEUS: I don't know.

PENELOPE: Come home.

ODYSSEUS: I can't. Not yet. I'm—I'm needed here.

PENELOPE: You're needed *here*.

ODYSSEUS: Nell you're breaking up!

PENELOPE: What?

ODYSSEUS: I'm losing you!

PENELOPE: ODYSSEUS?

ODYSSEUS: NELL?!

PENELOPE: ODYSSEUS?! ODYSSEUS!!!

(ODYSSEUS *disappears.*)

PENELOPE: It was so quick.
It all happened so quick!

PEGGY: *(From the loom)* Too quick! Too quick! All of it!

PENELOPE: I didn't know. I didn't understand.

PEGGY: It only gets quicker. Quicker and quicker.
Faster and faster!

PENELOPE: I can't seem to catch my breath.

PEGGY: So fast it seems like its all at once and all of a
sudden and out of time and—

PEGGY/PENELOPE: —out of breath!

PENELOPE: I'm out of breath!

PEGGY: Fight through it!

PENELOPE: I'm trying!

PEGGY: Try harder! Ask for more! Go deeper! Dig
deeper!

PENELOPE: I don't know how much further I can go!

PEGGY: Go until you can't go! RAGE!

PENELOPE: HELP ME!

PEGGY: HELP YOURSELF!

PENELOPE: WHY DID YOU LEAVE ME?

PEGGY: I HAD TO LEAVE YOU!

PENELOPE: I WANT YOU BACK!

PEGGY: I CAN'T COME BACK!

PENELOPE: COME BACK!

PEGGY: WHAT DO YOU SEE?

PENELOPE: RED!

PEGGY: YES!

PENELOPE: FURY!

PEGGY: YES!

PENELOPE: RAGE!

PEGGY: YES RAGE!

PENELOPE: FRUSTRATION!
LOSS!
LOST

PEGGY: RAGE!

PENELOPE: LOVE!
LUST!
Undo!
Undone!
I'm undone!
UNDO ALL OF THIS!
I WANT TO UNDO ALL OF THIS!
ALL OF THIS!
MY LIFE!
THIS!
THIS!
UNDO!!!!

(PENELOPE *starts shaking the loom. Breaking it.* LUCIUS *rushes to her.*)

LUCIUS: Penelope stop! PENELOPE!

PENELOPE: LUCIUS! LUCIUS!

PENELOPE: I'm—I can't breathe. I can't finish anything. I start something and then I think its horrible and I undo it and start again and then I undo that and start that again and I can't seem to get anywhere.

LUCIUS: It's O K, P, it's O K.

PENELOPE: It's not ok Lucius! It's not O K! It's shit! It's
all shit! I'm—

LUCIUS: You're not—

PENELOPE: I can feel all this stuff in me, this world
of—things, so close I can sometimes, I can get to it,
I've been there, to that place but I can't stay there, I get
scared, I pull back, I run away, I stop breathing and it
makes me feel crazy. And I don't want to feel crazy.
I want to feel—home. I want to feel like I'm home. I
never feel like I'm home.
You're so handsome.
You—you've been—I'm so happy you're here. And—
you're so good with him. With Telemachus. And me.
You're so good with me. You've changed Lucius.
You're stronger now. You've gotten stronger and I've
gotten weaker. I used to think I was stronger but I'm
not.
Sometimes I wonder what would happen if we kissed.
Sometimes I think we should make love. Sometimes
I think about that. About what would happen if we
made love. Sometimes I think about making love to
you. I think about what your body would feel like
with mine. How you would kiss me. How you would
hold me. How you would feel inside me. I think about
what you look like with your clothes off. I look at your
body through your clothes all the time. Do you look
at mine? You do. I see you do it. Over dinner or when
we're sitting on the couch or that day we went hiking
at Buttermilk Falls. Do you remember that day? It
was so hot and we jumped in the water really quickly
and then kept hiking. I know you were looking at
me that day. I could see that you were excited. I saw
you try to hide it. I let you hide it. I didn't want you
to hide it. I wanted you to take me the way you took

me that night at the Waterfalls years ago. That scared
me then but now its all I wish for. For you to take me
like that. Would you take me like that again? You'd
have to take me like that because otherwise it won't
ever happen. I can't let it happen. I can't be the one to
make it happen. It has to be you because I'm supposed
to be the one that's waiting for her husband to come
back. That's who I am. That's what people have made
me. That's what I made myself and I didn't mean to. I
didn't know that I'd have to wait this long or that the
waiting would turn into something else and that I'd
become this person, this woman with all this passion
and desire and love and soul and no way to get it out.
I would have done everything differently if I knew this
would be how I feel because Lucius I can't live like this
any longer. I can't live with all this inside me. I can't
live waiting for him to come home anymore. I need
release. I need to be free. I need to breathe. Will you
give me some of your breath? Will you breathe into my
mouth and give me back some life? Just a kiss. That's
all I need. A kiss would sustain me. I know it would.
That's all I need. A kiss. Will you kiss me Lucius?

LUCIUS: Penelope, I—

PENELOPE: Please. As my friend. As a man. Please.

LUCIUS: You're teasing me.

PENELOPE: I am not.

LUCIUS: Yes you are. You want me to kiss you and then
you'll go to your room and go to sleep and I'll be left
with all these feelings and no where to put them.

PENELOPE: Maybe you'll come to my room tonight. I
haven't let anyone in there in almost twenty years but
tonight, maybe I will. Maybe you'll sleep in my bed.
The bed you made for me. Under the tree, with the
stars over our heads. We could hold on to each other,
we could—be lovers, we could— Maybe tonight we

could. Maybe…but first you have to kiss me. Kiss me Lucius. Kiss me.

LUCIUS: Penelope I—

PENELOPE: I know. Just do it. Take me. Please!

LUCIUS: Once I start this, I won't be able to stop, I—

PENELOPE: I know.

(LUCIUS *grabs* PENELOPE. *Just then* ODYSSEUS *appears and pulls* PENELOPE *back into the past. We're at the airport. Their final goodbye)*

ODYSSEUS: Come on Nell, I don't want to miss my flight.

PENELOPE: We have time Odysseus, just—stop running from me.

ODYSSEUS: But I don't want to be—

PENELOPE: You won't, we're fine,

ODYSSEUS: Are you sure?

PENELOPE: I'm sure, just—stay for a second—

ODYSSEUS: Nell—

PENELOPE: Please Odysseus, I can't—you can't leave me in a rush, we have to—this has to be a real goodbye.

ODYSSEUS: It's not a goodbye baby, it's just a see you soon.

PENELOPE: Don't go Odysseus.

ODYSSEUS: Nell—

PENELOPE: I know I'm being selfish, I know, you're going off to do something important but all I want is for you to stay. You could still stay Odysseus.

ODYSSEUS: I can't Nell, I can't.

PENELOPE: What am I going to do without you?

ODYSSEUS: You'll be fine.

PENELOPE: How do you know that?

ODYSSEUS: Because I know you

PENELOPE: Do you?

ODYSSEUS: What kind of question is that? Of course I know you. I know you and you know me. …Come here…

PENELOPE: No.

ODYSSEUS: Come here Nell.

(PENELOPE *goes to* ODYSSEUS.)

ODYSSEUS: Look at me…

PENELOPE: I can't.

ODYSSEUS: Yes you can. Come on. Look at me.

(PENELOPE *looks into* ODYSSEUS *eyes.*)

ODYSSEUS: Penelope Johnson, you're my heart. And you always will be.

PENELOPE: I don't know what that means anymore.

ODYSSEUS: It means the blood that flows through my body is you. I am you Penelope. I'm you.

PENELOPE: You're me and I'm—

ODYSSEUS: Me. We're one.

PENELOPE: We're one?

ODYSSEUS: Kiss me Nell.

PENELOPE: No.

ODYSSEUS: One last kiss before I go.

PENELOPE: I can't.

ODYSSEUS: Nell, I need you to kiss me.

PENELOPE: I can't do it. I can't kiss you..

ODYSSEUS: Nell, this isn't how this should be,

PENELOPE: You're right, this isn't.

ODYSSEUS: Then make this right and kiss me.

PENELOPE: Just—go. Go. Leave. Go now

ODYSSEUS: I won't go until you kiss me.

PENELOPE: Then you'll never go.

ODYSSEUS: Nell—

(ODYSSEUS *grabs* PENELOPE, *starts to pull her into his arms. At the same time,* LUCIUS *appears and tries to pull* PENELOPE *into his arms. The two men struggling to hold her…*)

PENELOPE: Let go of me.

LUCIUS/ODYSSEUS: Never.

PENELOPE: Let me go.

LUCIUS/ODYSSEUS: I'll never let you go.

PENELOPE: This isn't what I wanted!

LUCIUS/ODYSSEUS: What do you want?

PENELOPE: I don't know.

LUCIUS/ODYSSEUS: You want me.

PENELOPE: No. I don't know. I don't know what I want. I don't know what I'm doing. Stop!

LUCIUS/ODYSSEUS: No.

PENELOPE: STOP!

(ODYSSEUS *turns into* TELEMACHUS *who is struggling with* LUCIUS, *trying to get* PENELOPE *out of* LUCIUS' *arms.*)

TELEMACHUS: Lucius!

PENELOPE: Telemachus?! Telemachus!

TELEMACHUS: PUT MY MOTHER DOWN!

(TELEMACHUS *jumps onto* LUCIUS, *wrestling him to the ground,* PENELOPE *falls as well.*)

LUCIUS: LEAVE US ALONE TELEMACHUS, THIS IS BETWEEN YOUR MOTHER AND ME.

TELEMACHUS: GET OFF MY MOTHER! GET OUT!

LUCIUS: Telemachus, you don't understand—

TELEMACHUS: GET OUT OF OUR HOUSE!

PENELOPE: TELEMACHUS!

LUCIUS: THIS IS MY HOUSE!

TELEMACHUS: GET OUT!

LUCIUS: I BUILT THIS HOUSE! I BUILT THAT BED!

TELEMACHUS: GET OUT!

LUCIUS: THAT'S MY BED! THAT'S OUR BED! SHE'S MY—

TELEMACHUS: GET OUT!!!!

PENELOPE: TELEMACHUS, LUCIUS, STOP!!!! BOTH OF YOU!!! STOP!

LUCIUS: Tell him Penelope, tell him everything. Tell him how you love me. How you've always loved me, tell him Penelope. Tell him so he understands. Tell him or even better, show him. Here. Here you can show him. *(He gets on one knee in front of* PENELOPE.*)* I've been holding on to this for so long now P, but I'm ready now, you're ready now, we're ready. Penelope, will you marry me?

*(*LUCIUS *has pulled a ring out of his pocket and holds it out to* PENELOPE.*)*

(Beat. Then PENELOPE *comes to* LUCIUS, *gets down on her knees in front of him.)*

PENELOPE: Oh Lucius, this ring is—

LUCIUS: I made it for you…I—

PENELOPE: It's…beautiful…

LUCIUS: …Put it on P, put it on and we can—

(PENELOPE *is just about to put to take the ring, when she sees* TELEMACHUS. *The two stare at each other and then* TELEMACHUS *runs off.*)

PENELOPE: Telemachus…

LUCIUS: It's O K, P, he'll—

PENELOPE: No, It's not O K.

Lucius, I—

LUCIUS: No. No. P. No.

PENELOPE: …Lucius, I—I'm…

LUCIUS: But I waited. I waited and—

PENELOPE: We've both held on so tight,

LUCIUS: No. No P, it's -—

PENELOPE: I need to let things go now.

LUCIUS: Not me. You don't have to let me >

PENELOPE: <Everything. I need to let everything go.

LUCIUS: But I don't want to.

(LUCIUS *grabs onto* PENELOPE *for dear life.*)

PENELOPE: You will… Goodbye Lucius.

(PENELOPE *pulls herself away from him.* LUCIUS *doesn't move.* PENELOPE *turns and goes to her loom.*)

(TELEMACHUS *finds himself at the waterfall. Upset, kicking the rocks, raging.* PEGGY *in the shadows*)

PEGGY: You rage Telemachus! You rage. Let it all out.

TELEMACHUS: Who's there? Is someone here?

PEGGY: I'm here Telemachus! I'm here!

TELEMACHUS: Aunt Peggy?

PEGGY: Yes! Yes it's me! Oh Telemachus! You can see me?

TELEMACHUS: Yes I can see you! But how can this—

PEGGY: Don't ask questions! Just touch me Telemachus! Take my hand!

(TELEMACHUS *reaches out his hand.* PEGGY *grabs it.*)

PEGGY: You're so warm… I'm gonna jump into your arms now, O K?

TELEMACHUS: O K.

PEGGY: O K, here goes.

(PEGGY *jumps into* TELEMACHUS' *arms. He cradles her.*)

PEGGY: You feel so good. I used to cradle you like this. And tell you made up stories about Ithaca. Do you remember that?

TELEMACHUS: Yes. And they used to all start out the same way.

PEGGY: That's right. Do you remember how they started?

TELEMACHUS: I think so.

PEGGY: Tell me a story now then Telemachus.

TELEMACHUS: (*Imitating* PEGGY) Of course that was a different time in Ithaca. A more magical time. Do you believe in magic? Oh I do, I believe in magic…and love. I believe in love. (*He can't go on.*)

PEGGY: It's alright Telemachus. It's alright. Hold on to that. Remember that. Do you promise to remember it?

TELEMACHUS: I promise.

PEGGY: Good… Now listen to me. And listen good. In just a second you're going to put me down and you're going to leave here.

TELEMACHUS: I don't want to leave you.

PEGGY: I don't want to leave you either but its time for me to let go now. (*Beat*). Now put me down.

TELEMACHUS: Aunt Peggy—

PEGGY/PENELOPE: Bravery.

(TELEMACHUS *turns and leaves* PEGGY *who starts to climb back up the rocks.* TELEMACHUS *sees* LUCIUS *who is still standing in the same place.*)

TELEMACHUS: You loved my Mom all these years.

LUCIUS: I did.

TELEMACHUS: That's why you built her this house. Is that why you wanted me to work with you—so you could get closer to her?

LUCIUS: No. Telemachus, I—

TELEMACHUS: You used me.

LUCIUS: No I didn't. I wanted to know you. And I wanted you to know me.

PENELOPE: *(From her loom, working)* Look at your life.

(LUCIUS *starts to walk away.*)

TELEMACHUS: Lucius!

(LUCIUS *turning to* TELEMACHUS. …)

TELEMACHUS: …See you around.

(LUCIUS *and* TELEMACHUS *walk off in opposite directions.* LUCIUS *walks to his guitar. Sits and starts to play*)

PENELOPE: Deeper.

PEGGY: Higher. Higher still. Reach.

LUCIUS: *(Starts out slow, plaintive)*
I want a recipe for
How to let things go
Four cups of feeling
A tablespoon of luck
Three dabs of my pain
And mix it all up.

PENELOPE: Bravery. Breathe.

PEGGY: Reach!

PENELOPE: Lost. Love. Lust. Rage. Fury. Ferocious. I can do this.

PEGGY/PENELOPE: Don't pull away!

LUCIUS: Add a
Sprig of history
Hope, just a touch
Let it simmer for some time
But not too much

PEGGY/PENELOPE: Let go!

PENELOPE: Let it all go!

LUCIUS: Cook this in a darkened room
Keep it hidden from view
When the aroma takes you over
You know your job is through

(*Music pauses as* ODYSSEUS *appears.*

ODYSSEUS: Your love is what keeps me alive.

PENELOPE: Your love has been killing me.

(PENELOPE *crosses to* ODYSSEUS *and kisses him… He disappears. She moves back to her loom, ready to work now.*)

LUCIUS: (*Music becomes more driving, insistent*)
Let the smell waft through the air!
Let it float high
Let it take others in
Let it let things die

PEGGY: Reach!

PENELOPE: Go! Yes! Go!

PEGGY: Let it all go!

PENELOPE: Fly!

LUCIUS: I want a recipe for
How to be reborn
Ten cups of hope

Twenty barrels of love
A sprinkle of past painAnd mix it all up

(PENELOPE's *loom begins to light up with a most beautiful light.)*

PENELOPE: Aunt Peggy, do you see it?

PEGGY: I do.

PENELOPE: Is that—

PEGGY: YES!

PEGGY/PENELOPE: Look at it!

PEGGY: That's a beautiful thing! Let it go!

PENELOPE: Let it go!

(*The light gets brighter and* PENELOPE *is taken by it...)*

PEGGY: Goodbye Penelope.

(PEGGY *turns towards the Falls. Walking to them slowly.* PENELOPE *begins to pull fabric from the loom. The fabric seems to go on forever and as the fabric pours out the world of the play begins to transform—into the world she's seen in her mind's eye before—the color of the waterfalls slowly growing and taking over the space.)*

LUCIUS: Add
A bunch of history
Hurt, just a touch
Cook it really fast
But not in a rush

(TELEMACHUS *enters. He stands far from* PENELOPE.)

PENELOPE: Telemachus.

TELEMACHUS: Mom.

PENELOPE: Come here.

(TELEMACHUS *won't come to* PENELOPE. *She comes to him, fabric in her arms.)*

LUCIUS: Set this out in the light
Let others see what you do
When they all ask for a bite
You know your job is through

PENELOPE: I'm here now Telemachus.

LUCIUS: Let them all have all they want

PEGGY: Fly!

LUCIUS: Let them get high!

PENELOPE: I'm here now.

LUCIUS: Let them share what you've made

PENELOPE: I'm here.

LUCIUS: Let them free to fly

PEGGY: Fly!

LUCIUS: Let them free to fly

PENELOPE: I'm your Mother, I'm Odysseus' wife, I'm a woman, I'm Penelope, I'm—

TELEMACHUS: Home!

PEGGY/PENELOPE/TELEMACHUS: I'm home!

(PENELOPE *tries to wrap the entire world in her fabric.* PEGGY *climbs towards the Falls, slowly becoming one with them.* LUCIUS' *music becomes faster and faster, more powerful, insistent as we—*)

(*Blackout*)

END OF PLAY